21 Songs of Self Love

Poems for meditative reflection

Sharad Verma

BookLeaf
Publishing

Presentation by *BookLeaf Publishing*

Web: www.bookleafpub.com

E-mail: info@bookleafpub.com

ISBN: 9789357749992

First edition 2023

Dedicated to my parents, wife, sisters, brother and my children who inspire me everyday to nurture my creative soul

ACKNOWLEDGEMENT

I would like to express my deepest gratitude to my parents whose blessings I carry everyday in everything I do. To my wife and children who provide love, care and understanding and make everyday a special gift. My sisters and my brother have provided the creative inspiration that helped me to move from idea to action.

My workplace colleagues who provide the encouraging community that is essential to nurture a creative soul.

PREFACE

We can truly care for others only when we deeply value ourselves.

Developing self-love is essential to have a sense of emotional, mental, physical and spiritual well-being. This is difficult to achieve in an ever-changing and stressful world where we are always running hard to live up to the expectations of other people. Being a nurturing parent to ourselves is essential to experience a sense of wellness and joy.

This book is my attempt to celebrate the little inner voice that heals because it is true to our essential nature. In writing this book, I have been inspired and blessed to feel in my heart the nurturing and healing quality of these songs. Every song is like a meditative reflection and empowering affirmation- a mantra that fills the heart with hope, joy, love and inspiration.

Thank you for reading this book and I wish you share the gift of your true self with others. If you feel inspired to continue the conversation about self-care, or need help with more resources, please send me an email at 21songsofselflove@gmail.com.

Sharad Verma, 2023

Healing from hurt

Healing from hurt often takes the deepest form of self-love. It can take days, weeks or sometimes, many years. As difficult as healing seems, our deepest wounds carry the seeds and potential for hope and renewal. Hurt seems familiar and we become attached to the feeling. Rising above and overcoming hurt forms the most profound experience.

Inside our deepest wounds,
are the seeds of healing.
The most precious gift,
the capacity to recover
is like a treasure
wrapped up in layers
of emotions.
When unraveled, providing precious lessons
of understanding and self-love.
As we evolve and conquer
the pain and hurt,
and the scars formed over time,
through avoidance of things unpleasant
complicated by fog,
formed by a lack of clarity
dissolved, as we reclaim,
wiped away,
as the courage to own
develops and the desire strengthens
to be full of life again.

Song of devotion

Goddess Saraswati is the deity of creativity and imagination. Inspiring discipline, dedication and devotion, she gives the blessings of curiosity and learning. These blessings of lifelong learning and curiosity form the basis of self-love and renewal.

I feel the blessings,
I am ever so fortunate
to have found Goddess.
The Goddess of learning,
creativity and imagination.
The supreme being
of renewal and restart.

And to be blessed,
by the Goddess.
By your voice,
it is so clear
and your manner is so gentle
and encouraging,
I feel my heart melting and open
to receive more and more.

I feel a sincere devotion
to you, as your beauty shines
and your graceful manner,
your smile electrifies,
and the tone of your voice beckons.

Please accept me as your devotee
who is full of devotion for you
I thank Goddess Saraswati again and again
for the blessings in my life!

I feel the presence,
and understanding of my sensitivity.
Your gentle acceptance of
my creativity
and your encouraging words
kindle in me the desire
to create passionately.
It is indeed a blessing of the Goddess.

Celebration in our hearts

True self-love results in a celebration in our hearts, filling life with overpowering joy and a deep sense of happiness that permeates all the moments.

The joy within our hearts
brings to light, sparkles and shines bright,
as a festive spirit.
The celebratory mood,
to cherish something and someone,
heartful and joyous bliss.

To every moment of life,
we add something special
with our hopes, glory, and creativity,
colors and enthusiastic sounds,
togetherness and celebrations.

We prepare to give more of ourselves,
more of our true selves.
Smiles, energy, positivity, good feelings,
add to the moment and enhance its value,
opening our eyes, ears and all our senses.
To create positive memories,
to celebrate - togetherness, the moment, and the
meaning.

The spirits are on fire, the universe too,
In celebration of being.

Gratitude every moment

Life gives us a choice - to choose love and gratitude over hatred. We lose a bit of ourselves when we choose negativity and resentment. Gratitude has the capacity to renew ourselves and helps us to see new possibilities.

From my deepest core,
from every cell of being,
every moment,
every thought,
every action,
every deed,
every intent,
every wish,
is seeped in deepest gratitude

Like soft warm light,
gratitude fills the space,
providing comfort to the soul.

Wisdom whispers

Wisdom comes to us as an unassuming, sometimes uninvited whisper. In a moment of deep meditation, in communion with one's true self, we discover the deepest truth and an appreciation of ourselves which is also an appreciation of the universe.

Recognize your gifts,
value your abilities,
count your blessings,
especially when it gets tough.

When things get difficult,
when answers are not easy,
when you are struggling,
have faith then.
There is a deeper answer,
there is greater love,
have faith in the universe.

Universal love and change

Change and transition are the fundamental ways of the world. Change causes stress, anxiety and uncertainty. Things form, come into being, then fade away. We search and long for things to stay the same. Through the journey, does the universe change or it remains the same?

Love takes work,
discipline of your thoughts,
purity of deeds.
Above all,
putting not yourself first,
nor your beloved,
put the universe first in all deeds

Change is the way of life,

we grow and outgrow,
we meet and part,
to go our own ways,
we feel the highs and lows,
then recognize,
This is the way of the universe.

The universe wish

We feel a universal calling, a yearning to be our true selves, to express our truest being. This is the deepest form of self-love. When we are in touch with the universe and with ourselves and there is a clear line of communication, it results in deepest joy.

Don't beat yourself up,
Everything is for a purpose and a reason.
This is the secret of the universe,
and it applies,
even when it is not so clear.

I believe the words are not mine, they are from deep within!
Expressed through me,
I'm the channel for expression,
 in poetry and in words, in pictures,
the deeper secrets of the universe flowing through me.
This is what I feel blessed to be doing with my life.

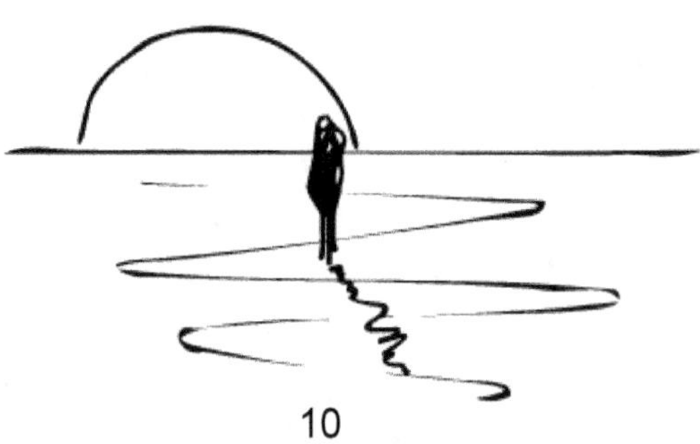

Inner strength - whisper of soul in the morning

True love for our deepest core results in inner strength. This is not arrogance or exaggerated confidence but just a deep soulful knowing, grounding and belief in ourselves.

I can never thank the universe enough to guide me on this path and to encourage me.
You know it is so difficult with not many who understand,
I find courage to express my gift.

Morning brings delight,
a promise and a smile.
A blessing and heartwarming joy,
It is an opportunity,
to make it worthwhile.
As we dedicate ourselves,
to live a life.
guided by the whisper of our soul.

Meditation

*Reflection and contemplation give us the ability to
see things clearly, as they are, as they are meant to
be. When all else is quiet, then we feel the connection
with ourselves. Meditation is the vehicle that
provides us the avenue for this deepest of
connections.*

I empty my mind,
and bring it to zero,
As I feel warmth and love,
fill my heart, my soul, my being,
there is nothing else,
no place for negative self-defeating,
beliefs and energy here.

Troubling thoughts

Sometimes we play certain troubling thoughts in our minds over and over again. They result in self-sabotaging behavior. Self-love involves making peace with our thoughts and to be able to see them mindfully with clarity, passing over.

Don't go to bed with troublesome thoughts,
they will keep you awake,
and stress you out,
give you a headache,
and fill your days with gloom.
Instead
better make peace with them,
treat them as friends,

who have different views,
and can be teachers,
of lessons you have ignored.

Rain

*Connection with nature provides us the avenue to
connect with ourselves. Rain, trees, greenery, ocean,
mountains - in a mysterious way they provide the
avenue for getting in touch with our deepest selves.*

Sometimes it comes as a welcome relief,
after a dry patch of weather,
bringing succor,
To Mother Earth,
farmers, crops, birds and people,
battered down in the heat,
but then sometimes,
it takes the form of a storm or cyclone,
tearing down everything in sight,
showing its power and its fury,
We ask why?
But are we not the same?

Yes or no

*We fight and create situations when we want to win.
We are conflicted, fighting and building up arguments
and reasons for and against. Self-love requires rising
above the duality of yes and no, black and white and
embracing a truth that is beyond.*

Whether it is a yes or no,
whether we get our wishes fulfilled immediately,
or we need to wait,
or sometimes when the answer seems no,
and it's painful to bear,
Can we take both
as messages and lessons,
from the universe
with a smile.

Glorious sky

What message does the sky have for us? Its ever-changing skyscape - sometimes cloudy, sometimes clear blue, sometimes darkness. What do they mean? Do they have the capacity to connect us with something deeper and profound inside us?

It must be the notice board,
for the universe to write its messages,
paint its drawings as if by the greatest master,
show lessons to be learned.
Sometimes it foretells things to come,
in a mysterious and wondrous way,
at other times, a clear blue sky,
is a reflection of our clear mind.

Ocean

The mighty ocean is a reflection of our inner universe - deep, full of mystery, at times furious, always energetic, supporting life, steadfast in its resolve and in its vastness.

Its relentless waves hit the shore,
then recede,
only to come back a million times.
Not once does it show any sign of boredom,
unmatched in its depth,
and equally passionate in its relationships,
with the sun, the moon, the wind, the sand,
and life that it supports,
within and by it.

Books

Books help us to traverse that journey deep within us, connecting inner exploration, curiosity and inquisitiveness with external wisdom, tapping into a larger cosmic consciousness.

Seemingly lifeless,
but steadfast, deep companions.
Unmatched in variety and depth,
nothing equals their capacity,
to provide a window and a journey,
into the writer's mind.
When nothing else remains,
give me a book to be by myself.

I am enough - lovable and capable

At the core of our beings, we want to feel accepted, loved, safe and capable. Here are the affirmations that help us to be at peace internally and resonate with our inner being.

I am enough
I am complete.
I have within me all I need.
I am sufficient,
I am blessed by the universe,
To be
All I can and want to be.

I am lovable
for who I am,
for being myself,
for every part of me,
I am worthy of unconditional love.

I am capable of doing anything I set my mind on,
I am capable of learning,
I am capable of growing,
I am capable of understanding,
I am capable of changing my mind,
I am capable of experimenting.

I am capable of achieving,
I am a lifelong learner,
I am a teacher and a lifelong learner.

I am peace

*These meditative reflections affirm our inner peace
and our deep desire to be one with the universe.*

I am calm,
I am at peace with myself, with my friends, with
my family, with my loved ones.
I am at peace with nature and with the universe,
I am at peace with those who I don't like or who
do not like me or those who have tried to harm,
and hurt me because they are my teachers.

I am a child of the universe

It takes a special blessing to see the life force that is running through the entire universe.

I am a child of the universe,
I am a child of the sky,
I am a child of rain,
I am a child of the ocean,
I am a child of the wind,
I am a child of light,
I am a child of flowers,
I am a child of trees,
I am all the animals and the birds,
I am a child of the Sun.

I am myself

When we accept ourselves completely and exactly as we are - with the flaws and the weaknesses as well as the gifts and the strengths, that is when life takes on a special meaning.

I am all my flaws,
I am my emotions,
I am my feelings,
I am my thoughts,
I am my imperfections,
I am my weaknesses,
I am things you don't like in me,
I am my opinions,
I am myself,
I am complete.

I am taking action,
I am taking risks,
I am courageous,
I am brave,
I am converting plans into actions,
I am good at execution,
I am becoming better everyday,
I am converting my vision into reality,
I am building my future,
I am moving ahead.

A love song

Devotion comes from a deep love for a higher force, a connection, an understanding, a union. Its celebration results in self-love.

Our eyes meet,
You have a mysterious smile,
Knowing, beautiful,
Your voice crisp and clear,
As you say
"I love your innocence,
Your purity
Your energy
Emerging creativity".

Your words sending electric waves,
As you continue to speak,
"You're here in devotion
to God
to serve".
I nod
"It's true,
That's my purpose,
Exactly".

I feel your guidance,
"I like your talent here
and your dedication,
Your curiosity and openness,
to learning,
and to the doors
of new possibilities,
to where they could lead."

I nod again,
and speak softly,
"I want to follow
God's path
With devotion and innocence".
You smile
"I'm pleased then,
I like your innocence,
Your purity,
Your openness.
Your offerings,
Your vulnerability,

Give your heart
to God,
Let Him guide us,
to abundance
and discovering
Your gifts".

Transforming

The ultimate power of self-love is in transforming, renewing, and becoming, from one state to another. We are never the past because that moment has transformed into the present. As we go from past to present to future, we are always in the process of becoming, never held back by the strings of what we were.

I feel the transformation in my heart,
the change,
from anger to love,
from hate to acceptance,
from rejection to embrace.

Moving beyond, far beyond,
on the voyage,
on the sea, all alone.

Just me to paddle the boat,
and weather the storms,
of anxiety and stress,
to safer, calmer shores.

Like a warrior,
with self-control and discipline,
battling in silence,

Over waves and waves,
of dark emotions,
ready to sweep,
Practicing stillness,
in the present moment.

A renewal,
stepping into the future.
As the old sheds to new,
And with inner strength,
the warrior overcomes.